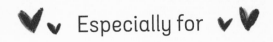 Especially for

With love from

THE BLESSING OF YOU

Copyright © 2021 by Mark Batterson and
Summer Batterson

Published in the United States by Multnomah,
an imprint of Random House, a division of
Penguin Random House LLC.

MULTNOMAH® and its mountain
colophon are registered trademarks
of Penguin Random House LLC.

ISBN 978-0-525-65387-5
Ebook ISBN 978-0-525-65388-2

The Library of Congress catalog record is available
at https://lccn.loc.gov/2020041570.

Printed in the United States of America

waterbrookmultnomah.com

10 9 8 7 6 5 4 3 2 1

First Edition

Book and cover design by Sonia Persad
and Annalisa Sheldahl
Cover art and interior illustrations by
Benedetta Capriotti

SPECIAL SALES Most Multnomah books
are available at special quantity discounts
when purchased in bulk by corporations,
organizations, and special-interest groups.
Custom imprinting or excerpting can also be done
to fit special needs. For information, please email
specialmarketscms@penguinrandomhouse.com.

THE BLESSING OF YOU

written by
MARK BATTERSON and
SUMMER BATTERSON DAILEY

illustrated by
BENEDETTA CAPRIOTTI

MULTNOMAH

Whatever you do, wherever you go,

there's something important that you need to know...

God is with you. God is for you.

The blessings of God are **all around you.**

You can go east.
You can go west.

Either way, you are **blessed.**

If you travel as far as Kathmandu,

God's goodness and mercy will always find you.

His blessings will follow
you **as you grow,**

from the top of your head
to your pinky toe.

You really don't have
to look very hard.

I bet there's a bunch
in your own backyard.

Or take a quick trip around the block,
and spy God's blessings on your daily walk.

So many blessings all around.

Can you **taste** them, **touch** them, **hear** them in a sound?

The food you cook.
That breath you took.

A hug from Grandma
and reading this book.

When you can't sleep
and don't know what to do,
count your blessings
two by **two!**

Like the smell of cookies
fresh out of the oven
and sharing giggles with
your favorite cousin.

Zooming around with a shopping cart.

Splashing your way through a water park.

The waddling walk of a silly goose.

That funny feeling when your tooth is **loose.**

God's blessings look different every day,
though maybe it doesn't feel that way.

But take a look up at the clouds in the sky.
The presence of God is always nearby.

It's the feeling of peace down deep in your heart

that you can reach for when things fall apart.

It's the feeling of wonder,
or perhaps even glee,

found way up **high**
in a climbing tree.

"What else?" you ask.
I'm glad you did!

Have you ever seen
a giant squid?

Even the silly things
God puts in place.

He knows what will
bring a smile to
your face.

If you'll open your eyes
to the joys all around,
so many blessings
wait to be found.

Then look in the mirror.
What do you see?
You are the blessing!
I hope you'll agree.

God uses your hands.
God uses your heart.
In His plan to bless others,
you play a **huge** part!

You have talents God uses to bless,
a unique personality you need to express!

Completely original, you're one of a kind.
Amazing ideas run through your mind.

When someone is **sad**,
they don't feel super,
you can bless them
with your sense
of humor.

When someone
is **scared**,
their thoughts
full of fear,
God blesses them
with your
listening ear.

When someone is **lonely**, feeling ignored, invite them to talk. Do they like to skateboard?

When someone is **happy**, they've done something great, give a high five and celebrate!

When you feel **high,** when you feel **low,**

you can bless others wherever you go.

You, my dear, have just what it takes.

So don't give up when you make mistakes.

You can love others in your own special way.

You can bless others with joy every day!

Hold this promise down
deep in your **heart:**

God has blessed you
right from the start.

How do I know that
all this is true?

The blessing of God is
the blessing of you.